W0017007

PANIC

PANIC

POEMS BY

LAURA MCCULLOUGH

ALICE JAMES BOOKS
FARMINGTON, ME

© 2011 by Laura McCullough
All rights reserved
Printed in the United States

10 9 8 7 6 5 4 3 2 1

Alice James Books are published by Alice James Poetry Cooperative, Inc.,
an affiliate of the University of Maine at Farmington.

ALICE JAMES BOOKS
238 MAIN STREET
FARMINGTON, ME 04938
www.alicejamesbooks.org

Library of Congress Cataloging-in-Publication Data

McCullough, Laura, 1960-
  Panic / Laura McCullough.
    p. cm.
  ISBN 978-1-882295-84-5
  I. Title.
  PS3613.C38645P36 2010
  811'.6--dc22
                          2010032290

Alice James Books gratefully acknowledges support from individual donors,
private foundations, the University of Maine at Farmington and the
National Endowment for the Arts. ❦

Cover art:
Julie Jalil, "La Panique"
2004, 16" x 20"
Oil on Canvas
www.jalilart.com

CONTENTS

PART III
WHAT BREATHES

ACKNOWLEDGMENTS

My gratitude to the editors of the following journals in which these poems or earlier versions appeared:

The Apple Valley Review: "Sun Dog, Moon Ring, Glory" (under the title "Light and Sound Are Not Opposites"), "The Predictable, Suspicious Tide," and "Waiting to See What the Weather Will Do"
Barrow Street: "The Necessity of Fire"
Blood Lotus: "Along the Surface" and "The Night, Saturday, Bridge"
Connotation Press: An Online Artifact: "Panic, Red Bank" and "The Semantics of Panic"
Ginosko Literary Journal: "How a Woman Can Look Beautiful Even when She's Stricken"
Harpur Palate: "Circle, Line"
Hiram Poetry Review: "Like a Virus"
Holly Ridge Review: "Severance"
Hotel Amerika: "What He Did with His Hands"
Iodine Poetry Journal: "Sea Bright, Sea Wall"
Iron Horse Literary Review: "The Inadequacy of Pink"
JMWW: "Bartering and the Myth of Shells"
Lips: "Chemical Language, Girlfriend"
New South: "Dissolution and Assemblage"
Painted Bride Quarterly: "The Ways Water is Used" and "Button"
Riverbabble: "Gone a Little Wild" (under the title "The Uneven Seam,") "Divergence," "The Tile Man," "Cancer Man," "Certitude and Exposure," "Stamina," and "Wind and Water, the Drowning"
Stirring: "Oxygen, Moon"

"Bartering and the Myth of Shells" also appeared in the *JMWW Anthology IV*

My thanks to Suzanne, Kathleen, Nancy, and Jennifer for comments during the earlier stage of this project. Thanks to Suzanne and Lori for the use of their space while drafting some of these poems (so long, Joplin). Thank you to Peter Murphy and the Sea Isle City writing crew. Thanks to Zoey Forney who first read this manuscript as a whole. Thank you to Kathy for our time working together in Montrose. Thank you, Mihaela, Carey, and Julia for your intelligence, insight, and editorial advice. Always, thank you to Michael Broek, for more than can or should be written. And to Stephen Dunn, to whom I dedicate this book, my gratitude.

For Stephen

Bring me the sunflower so I can transplant it
here in my own field burned by salt-spray,
so it can show all day to the blue reflection of the sky
the anxiety of its golden face.

EUGENIO MONTALE,
TRANSLATED BY CHARLES WRIGHT

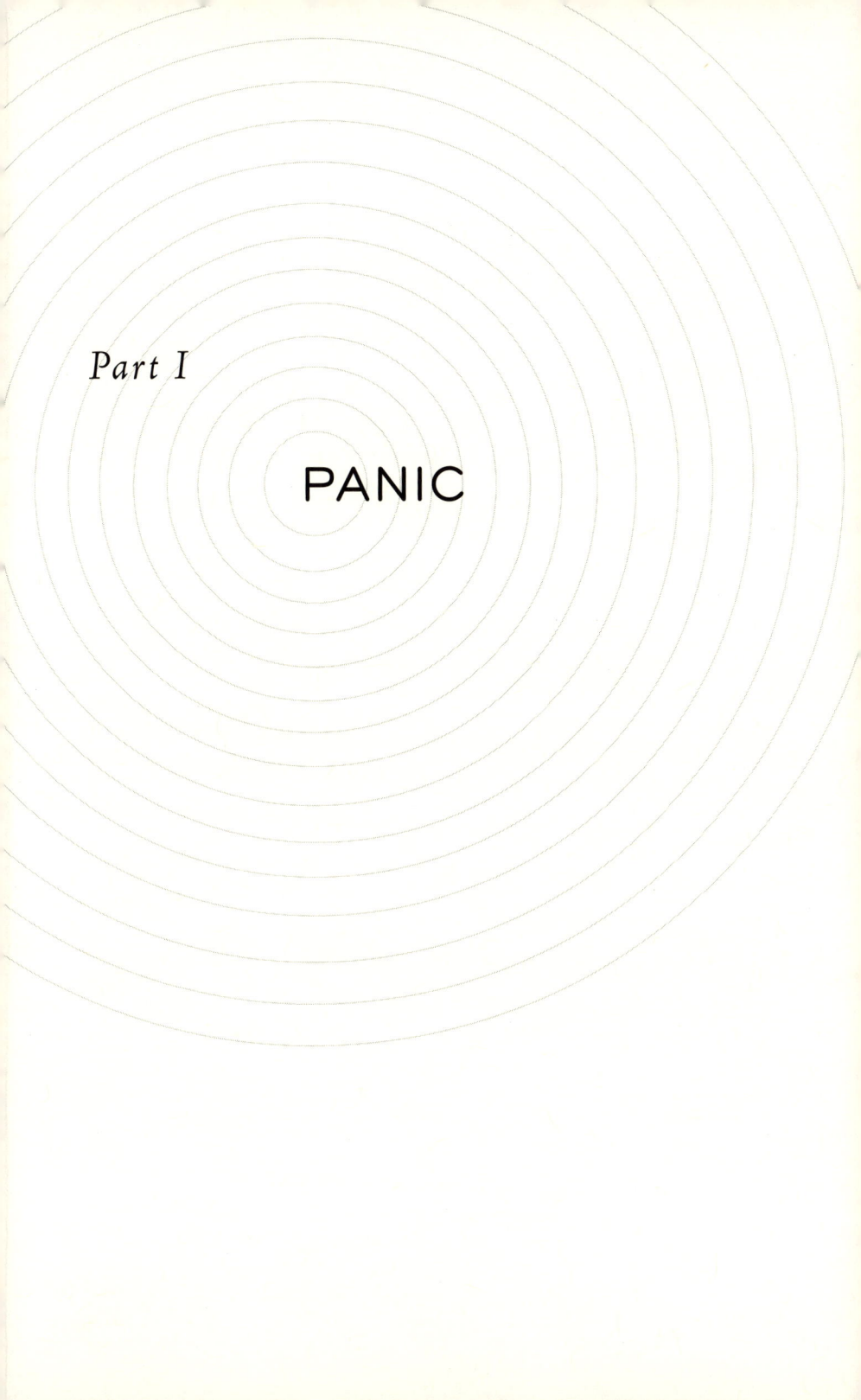

Part I

PANIC

DISSOLUTION AND ASSEMBLAGE

Down the street,
men congregate as if in prayer,
all stunned,
around one whose leg is trapped
between the girder and cement.
It is coming off.
Coming off, says one.
He is young, lured by the promise
of health benefits if he stays on through winter,
juggles school and work.

He could have been a lifeguard.
Sitting in the sun.
Checking out the babes.
The older workers—the men this life really belongs to—
have to decide what to do.

In the air, the sound of an alarm
and the smell of piss and asphalt.
Someone has let it go.
Maybe the man on the ground,
his mouth wide open as if he is trying to eat something
too big to fit inside himself.

There is no sound coming out,
but from his chest
a small motor is purring like a cat
working itself into a fit—
close to the pounce,
but not yet, not yet.

It is inside this moment
the men all fall in love with each other,
their wives and children dissolving as if in spirits.

The man on the ground will become their totem.
The boy in their midst
will learn this bitterness in his stomach
is something he can live with
and might even learn to like.

SUN DOG, MOON RING, GLORY

What is the opposite of decapitation,
a clean-through, laser-like amputation
of a girl's feet in midair
on a ride at the Sea Bright Pier?

They removed her to the hospital,
closed the ride.
The other customers were tortured
by the arriving media,
nearly begged to leave by the pier owners
who spoke to them each by phone later,
briefly as their lawyers had cautioned them:
Show sympathy; admit nothing.

The sun went down flanked by mock suns
in the moist twilight—
everyone
buying up the cheap hooded sweatshirts
to cover goose-bumps busting
from pink and burned skin;
everyone
hugging their chests,
trudging the boards against the night wind,

the sun dogs letting go, drowned in the bay.
Above them a cold moon ascended
sharp as a shucking knife
poised over a bucket of clams,

and later, the ring around it—
an optical phenomenon called a *halo*—
wondrous, the old wives' omen
for bad weather to come,

and down the boardwalk outside the Oxygen Bar,
kids playing with a hose,
spraying it and laughing
in the neon lights
oblivious to their cold, wet skins,
amazed at the *glory*
blossoming around their heads.

THE PREDICTABLE, SUSPICIOUS TIDE

The Lifeguard Captain didn't know there was a body
until a few hours later when the sun came up.
His four-wheeler's tracks leading to the rise
behind which she lay and then away.
He hadn't felt a thing, but she was dead,
her chest crushed,
the air flattened out of her,
lungs punctured,
her death a kind of drowning.

He was a smart guy,
flattered himself that he liked irony,
the collision of incongruous things,
even what approached paradox;
and sometimes
he'd let the young girls hang around his stand,
impress them with his knowledge
of philosophy and music,
tell them what to download to their iPods.

Often they would come again the next day,
say how beautiful this or that was,
and their eyes would be almost moist,
but he never took advantage of that,
preferring women to girls,
someone who might even surprise him.

But this?
How the mayor looked at him.
The reporters.
His suspension, pending resolution.
By then, there was no moon,
just the wide open sky, empty and suspicious
as he walked the beach,

hands deep in the pockets of his jacket,
head tucked low
against the slicing winds
and every invisible thing a night might contain.

CRAWLING LIVE AT THE BOTTOM
OF THE POOL

Along the rim of the baby pool,
a child balances one foot after the other,
her cream soles giving way to the creeping brown skin
that will not char in the summer sun.

Her mother watches her own feet,
toes painted silver, a toe ring glinting hot white.
She is oblivious,
her mind trapped between metal and flesh,
the articulated bones hidden in their cloth of cells.
She is unaware of her child
tipping this way over the shallow pool,
that way toward the aggregate of white sand and small stones.

Across the surface,
toys float, most belly-up.
The shadows' shadows crawl across the bottom
like undiscovered creatures,
alive and needing to feed.
The most interesting evidence the day offers is

these quivering pulses of unintelligent animation
on the surface—just a child's acquired toys,
some paid for,
others found, left behind, another child's loss;

or just empty plastic bottles and cups,
cheerfully colored,
surely toxic.

BARTERING AND THE MYTH OF SHELLS

The child bit into a water toy
shaped like a fish.
Her mouth sprayed full of tiny beads
like desiccated blood
or the cracked open egg case of an endangered beetle.
They were not at all like tapioca,
and she flexed her tongue and spit,
but could not get them out.
She wailed for her daydreaming mother,
who tripped into the pool
to scoop the child into the basket of her hips.
Down on her knees, she splashed chlorinated water
into her daughter's gaping mouth,
the beads blistering the surface
like bubbles indicating the existence of an underwater creature.

Below them, the shadows spread
like a dark rash across a sleeping fish's body.
Above them, clouds like gills.

And the guard hearing them,
leaning on the fence, asking, *Is she okay?*
The mother thinks the earbuds against his throat
look like shells
she wants to reach out and touch
with the tips of fingers
suddenly as foreign
as anemones
at the ends of her lithe and freckled arms
instead of hands.

The child against her tipped out hip
drapes over her breasts.
The small throb at her neck
is all that betrays the animal
caged there, trying to get out.

THE INADEQUACY OF PINK

The child lies with a towel beneath her.
The hibiscus splattered across her bathing suit
is the false color of innocence,
like the myth of tropical islands,
the imagined bartering of small shells for metal.

Pink is the color
of some tongues,
the inside of a conch,
a spot on someone's thigh after a scab has fallen off,

or the corners of a lifeguard's eyes.

After a long night away from the pool
on the beach at Sea Isle,
he imagines the new world
rising out of his lap,
remembering his last save,
a girl gone too deep
and the tube she'd slipped through—
how he'd waited for a crowd to gather around him,

but how they didn't,
not even the child's family,
who simply collected their towels and toys
and went home to make lunch
and go on with their day
as if nothing remarkable
had happened at all.

BUTTON

His hands felt like paws or flippers,
big and inarticulate,
as if shoulder sockets, elbow joints, and finger bones
had all fused in the August sun,
a kind of annealing.

And this is what he sees now
when he looks in the mirror:
a created thing,
a ceramic puppet
whose arms stand like glass stems,
whose hands burst flower-like from the tips.

If he waits long enough,
perhaps he will be visited by bees,
but for now, it is only ghosts,
the children he hears splashing behind him
as he retrieves his tilting guitar.

If you meet Buddha on the street, kill him,
he recalls someone saying.
He thinks a fly has landed on his chest
and brushes it away,
but it is nothing
but a fleck of thread
sticking from a button
head come suddenly loose.

GRAVITY AND WHAT WORKS AGAINST IT

Clouds—like fish fossils
and the record of catches
someone else's god has made—
scroll over the pool on the margin of the community,
dotted with blue umbrellas.
Above, seagulls push
inland from the shore,
heralding a storm
the Weather Channel has not yet announced,
and ospreys dance
their *pas de deux*
over the golf course lake
seeded with fish for the retired professionals.
Winged hesitation
forces their bodies back into the sky
against gravity.
Their tremble, the stutter, as if unsure
what action to take,
all part of the preparation:
the releasing of the body to gravity's demand,
the plummet,
the fish just below the brown and green surface
never knowing the strike's trajectory,
the inevitability of it,
the cold pierce,
its ascent into the sky something
like flight.

NOTHING IS DISRUPTED

He walks out the automatic door into the brightly lit night.
Someone else has left him alone
here on this planet of strangers
who weep for distant griefs.
This one,
he won't tell the waitress about.
All he wants is something delicious,
with good mouth-feel,
so he can forget what it feels like
inside his solitary skin.

He knows no one cares, but is stunned anyway.
The night goes on
as it always does,
but he can feel
the small muscles of his body
going tight,
sure to disrupt the large ones.

Where are the television cameras?
Or the imperceptible click of cell phones,
he thinks, the telling, the news?

If only there'd been a gun,
a code orange or amber,
someone threatened,
a terrorist, a theft, an unguarded package
left behind by a stranger
who didn't come from here,
who didn't belong,
who didn't understand what we are really like.

She brings him a plate, white, round, full.
She says, *Do you need anything else, Honey?*

He looks up at her. He has no idea what language
she is speaking, her satellite face blinking
in the black world he floats in,
hovering,
waiting to be pushed.

WHAT NEEDS TO BE DONE

Her mother's shit bag is full
and the home health care worker late.
There's no ignoring this.
I would have waited, said the mother, *if I could.*

The daughter is in her thirties
and has no children yet,
and so doesn't know
you are always the girl of your mother.
My girl, croons the mother. *I am so, so sorry.*
Her chair is old.
A new one will not be coming any time soon.
Soon, she says to the daughter,
you'll find something to take you away from me.

The daughter does what needs to be done.
She makes orange juice,
diluted as is necessary.
Runs a load of laundry.

She stands at the sink.

Outside, the humid air looks like an embrace.
The world is a country she does not want to enter,
preferring the relative safety
of her mother's central air,
the familiar odors
no matter how distasteful.
She says, *Mama, I'll never leave you.*
For now, she knows who she is,
and who she is
is sufficient.

WHAT SHE TOUCHES

She knows she is beautiful,
but no matter how taut her belly muscles are,
the white women will hate her
for her two piece bathing suit,
though it reveals
no more than the curve of her breasts,
and though the women will say things like
Latina, and
How lovely your curly hair is,
or, if very brave,
ask if her children are adopted or mixed race,
and offer how lucky she is
to have three gorgeous daughters
who tan
unlike their own
who burn.
It does not matter;
she has already given in
to hating them,
the daughters,
theirs and her own,
the women in their summer hats
and delicate armored bathing suits
that pull this way and that
to eliminate their acquired curves.
The fat below their buttocks stippled like oranges—
the only thing she likes about them.

She watches
as they lift themselves out of the buoyant water,
the dark star between their thighs
visible in this moment
when they have their backs to her,
and she touches the arms of her sunglasses,
pleased by their slender arc.

WAITING TO SEE WHAT
THE WEATHER WILL DO

She sat in the infertility clinic waiting room
with her adolescent son.
They'd driven in the dark here,
over an hour, the boy sleeping in the back,
his school backpack pillowed under his head.

He paged through *Sports Illustrated*,
National Geographic, Bon Appetit.
She looked out the window at the darkening morning.

A storm was coming, a heat brewing in the air
that didn't feel right.

Everyone in the room was staring,
the nurses buzzing the way only women can,
quiet, intense, not giving anything away.

Then the lights went out.

Oh God, someone yelled from the bathroom,
or was it from some poor woman
on a table having a procedure?
Emergency lights came on, not bright, but enough.

She put her arm around her son,
felt her belly full beneath her belt.
The clock over the window blinked.
The Weather channel says there's a tornado watch,
said a nurse loudly. No one in the room moved
to put down a magazine and pick up another.

Here? whispered the woman two seats away. *I guess anything is possible.*
The women smiled at each other.
That's exactly right, she said,
and her son's arm beneath her hand
seemed suddenly smaller and less muscled than it had before.

WHAT HE DID WITH HIS HANDS

He stood firm on two feet
with his hands clasped carefully
in front of him
and looked the guy in the eye
and didn't flinch
when they shook hands.
He'd said his own name, fully,
first, middle, and last,
and explained that he would work hard
and show up,
and that he could be depended upon
if only the man would hire him.
Which he did,
on probation, he called it.
That means, he said, *you gotta prove yourself.*
Maybe you do okay, I give you a small raise.
Fuck up once, though, you're outa here.

It was alright. He understood this.
That's the way things were,
except that things were always this way.
This is what he knew.
And that he would have to be different
from what he knew.
He left with his hands at his sides,
unpocketed
until he was a block away,
and then his hands found
the small lint pills and loose threads.

He just gave up then,
letting his hands hang naked in the air
at the ends of his arms,
fingers loose, small creatures

that did not torment or make him curious,
but his palms itched,
Like a sonofabitch, he said out loud
into the bluing shadows coming down around him.

Tomorrow, he would begin.

THE ANXIETY OF WATER

Once, he came upon a group of people
huddled in a corner of Club Panikon
and leaped above their heads,
his body landing across the closed blossom of them.
They broke apart,
arms like petals flailing,
and them scattering like shrapnel,
one against a wall, another across some steps
and then stepped on,
several into others who shoved or rolled into or piled against other bodies,
so that when he finally pushed himself up
into the empty space he'd made,
he couldn't help but give in
to laughter, relief in the chaos.
He demanded they call him Pan,
laughing every time someone said it,
doing a little dance move, a shuffle.
He liked the way it made his heart grind,
how the humidity coming off the Atlantic
slowed between the right sets of eyes,
how a body coming off the dance floor
could look like water,
how bodies moved like tides,
how smoke and haze made the world
easier to swallow.

SLEEVE

The asphalt came down hot and heavy,
and the boy who shouldn't have been working but was
flung his arm out too fast, too close,
and the physical force of it pulled him in.
The truck's hind quarters oblivious
like a bulky animal with a small brain,
the brains of the men he worked with
came alive in sizzling bursts over their synaptic pathways
as they realized he'd gone under,
how the road they were paving
spun suddenly out from them to the world,
a black aggregate snake
that would connect their lives forever after.

One reached his hand into the stinking pile
burning the skin up to the elbow,
his screams the only ones anyone would hear,
since the boy was already dead.
The man who tried to save him
was pulled back by the others,
his skin bubbling,
the tattoo across his smoking bicep
depicting a woman laced in a spider's web.
It was clear she was meant to be beautiful,
but it was less clear
whether she was dangerous or in need of rescuing.

Later, he would come to like
the topography of the burned arm,
how the scars deepened into something
no one could have created for him;

he would joke that it was free,
this sleeve,
a map of a world
very few people ever enter.

For Peter M.

PANIC, RED BANK

That night the girl who passed out
from mixing alcohol with prescription drugs—
the names of which were not released in the papers—
died choking in her own vomit.

She'd danced.
She was pretty.
No one remembered she'd gone to the bathroom
until they found her in the stall.

He was outside on the curb,
his feet lined up artfully,
pencil pants bleeding into sneakers,
the foundation of a panoply
he contemplated
as the ambulance light chiseled
through the slag night.

When they took her away,
he went around the corner to the comix shop,
Jay and Silent Bob's, and leaned against the glass
looking in for Buddy Jesus
way in the back
thumbing up the town, the whole world.

Then he went next door to the Sweet Shoppe
and bought a cone with sprinkles
and sat on the bench out front under a street light,
one leg crossed over the other, white toe
swinging fast,
a cigarette in one hand, his ice cream in the other,

touching first one and then the other
to the skin
of the wrist
on the opposite hand.

THE SEMANTICS OF PANIC

The New Year's Eve fireworks were over,
everyone funneling away from the river's edge,
when the Red Bank police had to close the alley,
the police on either end saying,
It won't be long; there's a VIP convoy.
This didn't help the stranded party-goers,
all seventy of them,
especially those squeezed along the brick walls
or stranded in the sea of the very middle—
a log jam after a hurricane has set everything loose upstream,
garbage mixed with vegetation,
a rising swell—
and though it was no more than twelve or thirteen minutes,
hot spots began to fester:

the man who swung his arms wide
to create a space for himself,
then another man screaming,
and a punch thrown over by the wall,
the cops at both ends yelling,

and the woman who closed her eyes,
eased her body against the back of the man in front of her,
how he leaned forward a little to hold the weight,
let it fold over him like a warm cloak.

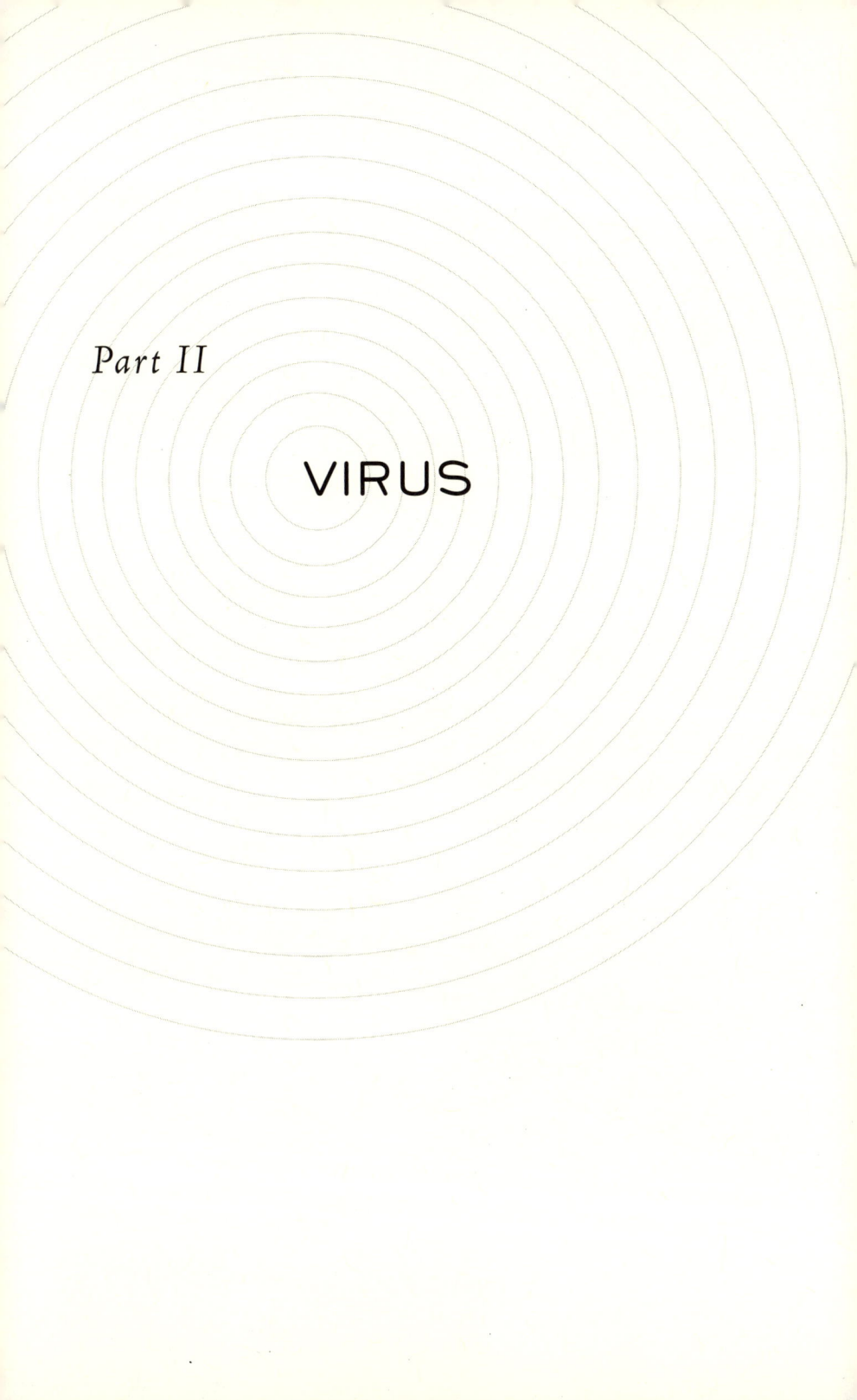

Part II

VIRUS

WHAT THE LIFEGUARD WROTE

That day,
the metal held the heat
and when the children's bare feet
slapped the surface, the skin crisped against it,
and they fell sideways over the edge to the mulch's
obnoxious embrace, small prints left behind and smoking
with residue. This happened not once, but three times, each time
the child's parents calling to complain and request a sign be put up.
He wrote a warning
on the inside of a pizza box
and staked it to the closest tree, though
all he recalls of the events before the drowning
is how he walked around the pool asking if anyone
had a pen, how one of the mothers lent him her lipstick
to write the word WARNING both large and red and how satisfied
he felt
both aroused and indicted.

COLLECTION POCKETS

There was a guitar that day,
but the lifeguard hadn't been playing.
In fact, he wasn't even on duty.
He'd stopped by to get the phone he'd left behind
when his shift ended,
and the guard on duty asked him to, *Hang there a minute,*
so he could *go take a piss* which he had to, he said, *wickedly.*
It spread the blame around a little, but it didn't matter.
The boy's body at the bottom of the pool suddenly,
then floating toward the surface,
arms out, legs dangling.
The coroner said he'd hit his head on the bottom,
yet no one saw him take the dive.

The lifeguard who was not on duty
struck the water the same time the boy's mother did
and had to wrestle him from her.

The trees' leaves all turned over like a storm was about to blow through.
The music inside him ratcheted up as he pressed the white chest
with his crossed palms closing down
against the mother's cries and the children splashing
in the water just inches away, coming within arm's reach,
desperate to see all they could.

Between the concrete squares, a pale gray marine epoxy lay smooth,
and nothing grew, no weeds, and there were no cigarette butts or bugs.
Only in the collection pockets of the pool.

THE NECESSITY OF FIRE

The anxiety of the golden faced boy burnished red
against his copper-plated chest as he bent
over the blue-tinged water, a tidal sadness coming

in, a season coming on unexpectedly. The strobe
red of the ambulance, the lights of the police cars,
men with nothing else to do, hands hooked in belts,

chests cocooned in thick blue, standing near as if he
were a sapling stupid enough to have cracked its seed
in a thicket of oak trees that understood each other's

need for space—how light must be trapped at the top,
and the necessity of fire to burn away what grows
in the underbrush, dangerous if not kept in check.

CHEMICAL LANGUAGE, GIRLFRIEND

She brought him a sunflower
from her mother's annual row,
this year scraggly—most halting
before the top of the fence, only
a few with heads enough to bow—
the stem thick as a tennis racket;
and he took it, the seeded eye
faceted like a fly's, the scrabbled
fiber of the petals dragging against
his palm. It had been two weeks.
She smiled from her two piece
bathing suit, the stud in her belly
inches from his hand, a star sending
light out across a universe. They
were bodies orbiting around nothing
but themselves. When she turned
away, he watched the small moons
of her shoulders and resented how
they seemed to whisper to each other
in a language he couldn't understand,
his own suddenly a mute chemistry
of muscles speaking only in adrenalin
and the universal dialect of disgrace.

LIKE A VIRUS

The twenty-five or so people
that she would call real friends
were not the first to respond

when she texted them, and many
didn't even live in the same town
or even the state, but said the same

things, *That's so sad; OMG, really,*
that's like awful, and when the "real"
ones—most of whom she had met

in "real life"—found out, it was like
that old game of telephone: what
began as, *A boy drowned at the pool*

my boyfriend is a guard at became,
A kid was trying to drown another kid
at the pool, and her boyfriend had to

punch him in the head, but only saved
the one; the other died until it became,
Her boyfriend was drinking while working

and this little kid drowned, and the mom's
got a lawyer and the guy's in jail with like
a million dollar bond, and her friends'

texting became a long error message
that often ended the same way, *And like*
how are you feeling? Are you breaking

up with him or something? And all she
could do, finally, was turn it off, put
it under her pillow, the moonlight

slipping through her blinds like a virus
making her skin feel suddenly as if it might
slip off and simultaneously as if she might

suffocate in it if it didn't. The image
of a body splayed like a frog in water
blue-white like a screen empty of text.

SCATTERED

Her towel and bags and her son's things
were all by the shallow end where she preferred he swim,
but she had come to sit by the deep end to smoke,
and how could it happen in less than half a cigarette's time?
The white tube between her stained fingers leaving her hand,
arcing toward the weeds by the fence—
the landscaping hadn't been maintained well this year,
a scattering of garbage here and there;
hopefully nothing combustible.

Could she really have thought about that?
she considered later,
replaying the event
in case it hadn't happened,
in case he was coming home soon
from his friend's house or the basketball court
or the stupid hump of dirt the kids all rode their bikes up and over,
the place they called The Jumps.

He'd broken his arm there the year before,
coming out of the woods,
his helmet askew,
the smell of him still boyish, but promising more.
She'd been angry for years
at this jumping, squirming, flailing, rowing away,

and here he'd gone under and away,
and she smoking and jumping in too late.
Like smoke clearing or a storm gone

leaving
a scattering
of broken branches and wet leaves
staining the concrete,

and no amount of bleach or scrubbing
will ever get it out.

HOW A WOMAN CAN LOOK BEAUTIFUL
EVEN WHEN SHE'S STRICKEN

How many times had he'd told the story?
The dead boy's mother, her face blossoming
out like a sea creature underwater,
and his own mother's face a moon,
saying, *I am so sorry for your loss*, in one breath
and *My son did the best he could* in another.
The air around them viscous, and all of them floating
in it like sea life, tide in, pools all full,
lawyers talking to each other amiably,
the Association president knitting her hands together
then laying them flat on the table,
then together again,
then prising them apart
as if they were children,
as if they were attacking each other in a mock war,
as if whining,
Someone's going to get hurt if you two don't cut it out,
might actually stop them.

WHAT MIGHT LIFT HIM

He played guitar at the funeral, the boy's mother sighing loudly.
You could be my son, she said, and this wrenched his brain
and made him angry, but he hugged back when she embraced him.
She was pretty, he thought, and this made him wish for his father
to be there next to his own mother. He'd been a butcher
at the local Acme and a lifeguard in his summers as a kid.

Once, he'd told the story of saving an eighty year old man from a rip tide.
The guy was old, but strong, an ex-marine. I had to knock him in the shoulder
to get him to quit thrashing. Got him in though. Never said thank you.
Then he'd punched the boy gently on the shoulder.
The best part of guarding is the babes. On the beach. Chicks. But don't tell your mom
  I said so.

The funeral was long, and he listened to his own breathing,
counting how many he'd taken. Sometimes he held it,
letting it out slowly, flaring his nostrils
while dipping his head to anyone who looked his way.

STAMINA

The cop who'd pulled him over
stood in the brake light's glow
writing him a ticket,
and without words downgraded the offense
to one with no points.

Perhaps it was the sunflower
gone leathery along the high ridge of his back seat
or the way the light caught his curls.
Or just his name.
Or that he was only a boy.

It might have been her sixteen years of rejecting the unsmooth moves,
the rude passes that almost passed for assault,
the way she always doubted her own strength and stamina,
believing sure exposure lay just ahead,
arriving any day now

if she didn't keep her mouth shut
and do everything,
almost anything,
that had been asked of her.

CIRCLE, LINE

That day, six seniors from the assisted living
center sat at the community pool.
One was on his oxygen, the tank parked next to the plastic recliner
with a blue towel draped across it for comfort,

and he'd seen the boy dive into the shallow end,
and there were signs. A circle. He remembered what a circle was.
A tiny man diving in a slim arc. A line cutting across.

Like No Smoking. He wanted a cigarette hot in his lungs
and cold menthol in his mouth,
the small ripple across his skin from the nicotine,
and the clarity—so temporary—his mind filling like lungs with smoke;
even in this air, next to the pool
next to the lake with the optimistic fountain,
even with the twin plastic nodules in his nostrils,
his arms placed along the chair rails, his hands dangling,
twitching the index and middle fingers of each against the other,
back and forth,
the drag on his skin reminding him to stay awake if he could,

the darned boy
an annoyance
going by again and again with his wet slapping feet
and scuttling run, then the sound of the sirens coming closer;
then the fear;
surely they would take him away for good this time.

WIND AND WATER, THE DROWNING

There was a moment
when the boy knew something had happened,
an inarticulate sensation,
animation
coming to an end,
his body becoming
what gives itself over—
buoyancy,   the limbs
the torso,
dulling light,
dimming vision,

but a face underneath him   asserting itself

arms encircling him   knowing, knowing
but unable to feel then a newness   as if

extinguish   became   *transfer*

to the water   spreading out

and this passed through the older boy
who was pushing the discarded body
up and out,

and the air was a plane over which *something* fled,
away from the lifeguard's anguish,
nothing more to be done

the mutable winds and waters
stirring and going still,

leaving behind requirements and consequences,
wearing everything else away,
creating shorelines and islands,
and covering, again, the humiliated sky.

THE TILE MAN

Each year it got worse: cracks
along the concrete sunbathing area that had to be patched;

areas around the coping
darkened by mildew that, no matter how much he bleached

and scrubbed, had gone
black; decorative blue sunburst tiles edging above the water

line (and often below
after a hard rain) lifting and popping out here and there;

and now the aggregate lining
beginning to degrade, patches across the bottom flaking off.

That's what happened
with these kind of pools; it was natural, but the Association

didn't like it,
and he'd noticed this year everyone was giving up a little:

nobody weeding around the flowers,
crab grass growing up in the seams, especially around

the baby pool behind its fence.
That was the worst area—the lifeguards never closing the umbrellas

left splattered with bird crap,
parents leaving food under the tables, wet diapers, juice boxes.

The tile man dipped a cloth
in the pool and wiped it across a plastic table mottled with dried

ice cream. He yanked
a snaking grass shoot, tossed it over the fence, then bent over

the shallow pool, still
as a mirror reflecting the baleful and broken sky.

Part III

WHAT BREATHES

CANCER MAN

He thought if he could just tell everyone
everything he knew about colon cancer,
he might be able to save someone,
and so this had, in his retirement,
become his hobby, his calling, his job,
he joked, *A dirty one, but someone has to do it,*

and he visited people in the hospital
and started a prayer group
and a MySpace and Face Book and a blog
and even uploaded a short video discussing the necessity
of frequent colonoscopies
for those with certain genetics on YouTube,
which actually got a lot of hits
because he was affable and self-deprecating
and looked a lot like Santa or Walt Whitman
depending on one's sympathies.

And he delivered pizza.
They needed him; he knew the neighborhoods,
and he didn't get too upset when stiffed.
That's life he would say,
or *They looked so poor, I thought I should give* them *some money.*

When he asked his daughter to use her phone
to video his next colonoscopy, so he could upload it
to show how easy it really was,
the family thought he was losing it.
There have to be boundaries, some limits, they pleaded,
but he said, *This is all I've got. It's who I am, and what I have to give.*
The daughter, of course, said no,
but when the father finally died,

his funeral was packed, the calls and emails flooding in—
most from people he'd never met in person.

New posts to his now unattended blog:
He was there for me when my husband died;
He prayed with me for my son's recovery;
He sent me daily emails when I was having chemo.
This, the record of their father's strange intimacies
in the virtual world, a second life
that wouldn't end with his physical one,
a source of ongoing embarrassment for the family
who stalked the site, but never posted,
not even once.

ALONG THE SURFACE

In Sea Bright early this summer,
a fisherman gutted a pregnant female Mako on the beach.
The crowd leaned against each other,
a tightening coil,
to see better as the babies slipped out on the sand.
When one flipped its tail—
so it seemed to jump toward a child—
a father stepped on it,
squashing its head,
apologizing at first, then getting angry
when his girl cried out.

Another name for a school of sharks
is a shiver,
which is what rippled along the surface of the water
as the evening wind blew across it.

The people left as they got bored,
some men wanting to help carry everything away:
the carcass, jaw,
and what remained useful, at least, as chum.

FISHING FOR ELVERS

Baby eels travel far and for years—

and the cars back in,
a man behind each wheel, ready just in case,
the others with their funnel nets down near the pipe.
And coolers packed with ice.
So much money suddenly,
a good market; they'll do it as long as they can,
as long as the Red Bank police don't troll by.

On toast, that's how he likes them,
but he won't take any home;
his buddies and he will do this five, six hours,
hand them off, and maybe hit the diner for eggs and potatoes.
Sitting there, wanting a smoke
and not being able to light up,
he'll step outside,
the last of his friends to still do this,
and the only one not yet out of high school,
kept back twice,
and no plans for afterwards either.

The neon of the diner fades.
He stares up into a sun he doesn't believe in,
the dark swelling in his pants' pocket
where the wad of this morning's money is bunched
barely keeping the panic down in his throat.

He looks at the small sun of the cigarette's ember;
he looks at the tattoo on his forearm—
the smoke swirling out of his mouth—
Midnight, it says in script,
the letters rippling over the ropes of his muscles and tendons.

He burns
one letter out because he can.
He wonders
if he can stand to burn them all.

THE NIGHT, SATURDAY, BRIDGE

The mound was a green sea turtle—
dead, her flippers stiff,
head elegantly bent,
the carapace a swirl of green and gray and black,
a signature for sure.
The children who found her
tried to tip her over
until a mother yelled, *Don't touch it; it could have germs,*
and then a kid used a stick to jab her flipper
to see if she would bleed.

The boardwalk lights that had been blinking invisibly
in the glare of the white sky
were revealed as night came;
the same night two teens,
a boy and girl, would be lured away,
the boy tied up, the girl raped,
the perpetrator fleeing the dry town of Ocean Grove,
taking the Garden State Parkway
either north or south,
and never caught.

It's all anyone talked about all week,
the turtle, the rape; then Saturday came.
The mayor was glad;
then the bridge between the island and mainland
got stuck open due to the heat,
and it was something to see,
the long snake of cars,
the air rippling above them.

CERTITUDE AND EXPOSURE

At the start of Sandy Hook, two towers stand,
a panopticon of the Jersey Shore,
New York's amputated skyline one way,
the sea down to Wildwood the other,
and inland—
houses, roads, Princeton whispering its serious talk—
and the school trip late in the year,
the heat already setting in,
and so many students certain their lives will really start in the fall.

The teachers and parents sit in the shade on the periphery,
looking out over the heads
of the students sitting on towels in the grass.
They don't want to make the climb
up the towers for the better view.
They just want to sit here
in the blistering sun
letting it touch them all over,
seeing how much skin
they can get
away with exposing.

LOOKING FOR PERMISSION

They got stuck in the Shrewsbury River,
having followed fish schools in,
and then didn't leave,
and the fall came
and then winter,
and things got bad.
People try. They try hard.
Some loved the dolphins,
gave them names,
went out on their boats and left them fish,
came closer than is legal.
That is how people are.
Wanting them to go;
wanting them to stay.

When the river started to ice over,
officials finally took action,
chasing the dolphins with State boats
hoping they would follow the open waterway
to the Navesink and then on to the Atlantic.
Some did; others went under the ice and drowned.

In Sea Bright, where the dolphins passed in and out of the ocean,
there is a bar called Dolphinhead,
the house drink: blue gin with mango foam.
The walls are painted fuchsia,
and they have karaoke every night.
There, in the black-lit dark corners,
someone asks someone else
to say something
true and beautiful.
It is the bar's tradition,
and once someone answered, *Only what dies is exquisite.*

He was given a lei, a free Dolphinhead, and the chance to sing.
The others silently mocked him—
no one so easily satisfied anymore,
wanting instead something perfectly imperfect,
the potentially dangerous,
permission
to display anger in public.

GONE A LITTLE WILD

It was her twin who died this unlikely way:
an uneven seam in a concrete pad,
the forklift tipping,
and bad luck
that made her fall the way she did,
her head caught between the metal canopy and the floor.
We agreed when the sister asked for,
and was granted by the mayor,
the right to plant a garden at Five Corners,
a circle in the center around which cars sped.
It was a nice garden,
full of coneflower, butterfly bush, and lilacs.
We'd see her out there watering,
and we'd slow down as we ran over the hoses she'd rigged,
cutting off the flow as we did.
When she asked to put up a sign
with her sister's name on it,
she was told no; too personal for a public space.

She no longer tends the garden—

the lilacs each spring mad with purple bundles,
and the coneflowers spill over the concrete rim,
their wide-petaled heads jutting out over the dull asphalt
as if grasping for us
as we speed by
in the citadels of our cars.

LIKE CRAWLING THROUGH A FIRE

In the comix shop,
she contemplates another tattoo,
one that might memorialize what she's come to know as truth.
It's her own beauty coming on
after so long thinking she was ugly—
how the sunburst around her belly
made her feel luminous until the winter,
how the small snake coiled around her thumb
scared off the encroaching lack of empowerment
only until she saw someone on the boardwalk
with the exact same thing.

Now she considers womanhood
and how maybe tattooed make-up—lips and eyeliner—
would free her from the morning ritual
of a magnifying mirror.
She tells her boyfriend this
as he breaks the spines of new Manga.
His low slung pants look transitory.
His pocket hangs open, and she puts her hand in.
The smile he gives her is like oxygen in a smoky room.
She closes her eyes and tries to breathe.

WHAT THE TEACHER SAID

He has returned to college,
but summer has changed him.
Once he walked around the edge
of an Olympic size pool,
balancing only on the bullnose,
swinging his arms out,
not falling when he stepped over the clean water pipe,
not even tilting when he stepped over the stile of the diving board,
pastures of concrete on either side.
This dead summer feels like a stile he has not crossed,
leaning instead over it, unable to find his balance,
just standing there like an animal
reaching thick lips through a fence
for the tall brown grasses.

He is here, but has left his guitar at home.
In class, a teacher posits,
In the collusion between image and syntax,
is sound and sense, and he wishes for neither,
and gives only monosyllabic responses to the worn out questions,
What did you do over the summer?
And *What will you be when you grow up?*
Which is never how they say it anymore,
careful to not insult the young and callow
who never think they are young and callow
because if they did,
they would falter in the wind they move so haphazardly into;

instead they let themselves go as dumb as cows,
so they can survive the pastures they must cross.

DIVERGENCE

There'd been two baby deer
in the yard for weeks;
no sight of the mother,
and then one of the fawns disappeared.
He'd been leaving apples and sweet potatoes
just like he knew not to do.
Take no action, all the articles read,
unless you've seen the body of the dead mother yourself.
She's around somewhere.
He hadn't, but now there was just one fawn
and the question was whether to catch it
or call somebody to come and get it.
Like the woodchucks last year,
which cost him hundreds
after they'd eaten fifty dollars worth
of annuals overnight.
The baby deer ate his hostas to the ground,
but he didn't seem to mind so much.

He contemplated the white spackling
across its slender, bony back.
How it would fit just under his hand,
the ridge of shoulder,
and if he squeezed, the legs might splay out,
the tiny enameled hooves shining
like diverging black opals.

So vulnerable, such creatures, he mused,
feeling suddenly protective again.
He was thinking only for himself—
not for anyone else,
not the neighbor's kids who'd named the fawns Click and Clack,
not the wider moral matter of urban encroachment—

just about his desire
to watch and consider
what it might be like
to hold its ribcage against his own,
see up close the spots
he knew would disappear
if it managed to survive.

THE MOMENT BEFORE SOMETHING

Her boss said,
You must be feeling better;
you're not talking about your dad so much anymore.
It had been a year,
maybe longer,
and the days had finally started to make sense again.
No need to leave notes on the night table:
Now get up, then go to the bathroom.
Brush your teeth.
Eat something.
She followed her own orders written down like that.
The kids lived like they owned the place,
coming in at reasonable hours,
not talking about where they'd been.
They weren't in trouble.
Grades were good.
They had nice friends and jobs
that gave them gas money and let them eat out often.
It was like having roommates,
ones who didn't mind her disappearing for a year
from their lives. They even, in a way, understood.
Grandpa had died. It was sad. You go on.
A month into the grief,
her daughter said it was cool she'd finally lost the weight.
She hadn't noticed the change
in her relationship with her boss
until he asked her out on a date.
I thought you might be ready, he said, and *We get along so well.*
She considered this.
It hadn't been easy as a single mom,
and he'd been good to her
when she had had to leave early or call out
when the kids were little.

Now, there was college just ahead.
She made a list of the reasons
to go and to not go.
The number in each column
was exactly the same.
There was no cemetery plot for her dad,
and she'd dumped the ashes months ago at the beach.
She put on the headphones to the iPod
her children had given her
full of *Four hundred songs we downloaded for you, Ma.*
She ran her thumb around the circle
like they'd shown her,
watched the titles slip by one after the other,
made a choice,
and waited.

DERACINATION

Sometimes the mother
of the kid who'd drowned
would come in
while he was there.
She'd say hello.
Sometimes tip him.
He couldn't think what it was like,
but he'd lost both his parents,
and his sister hadn't been the best at raising him;
he knew about being alone.
He never said this to her,
but felt bad taking her money,
and then after a while
didn't mind.
One day, she was standing in an aisle
looking down at the floor for a long time.
He knew it wasn't right
and stood near her, hands in his apron.
She finally noticed him, nodded, and smiled.
Once, he'd smashed her car windows.
Not just hers, but three in the neighborhood.
He knew it, and she didn't.
Now, he was going to do something with himself.
He took his hands out,
and asked if she needed help,
and when she put her palm against one of his,
he later described it as a little like being hit by lightning,
and his knees bowed
as if hit hard from behind,
so she reached to catch him
from falling instead of him catching her,
which is what he'd expected
and never came to pass.

THE GIRL IN THE HIBISCUS SPLATTERED BATHING SUIT

It is the last year she will wear it;
she is nearly five.
Her foot hurts, but she has enjoyed the treats
her mother and father
have both given her:
first a lollipop, and later, ice cream.
Her parents have been arguing downstairs.
Something has made them upset.
Her foot. The playground.
Something about a lifeguard.
They whisper.
She can't decipher.
Next to her is her Mommy doll and her Daddy doll
for when either of them are traveling for work.
In the next room,
someone has left the television on.
She goes in, walking gingerly on her hurt foot,
and sits on the floor.
It is a show about whales.
She's glad to still be in her bathing suit,
thinks of swimming with the whale,
riding its back,
holding her breath under water.
Then her father is at the door.
Who left the goddamned TV on again, he says,
and she looks up;
she knows she hasn't done anything wrong
and lifts her arms to him.
He takes her up, her chest against his,
and she says, *I can feel you breathing, Daddy.*
He squeezes, and she hugs back hard.
Then her mother has her arms around them both.

The father says,
For the first time, I'm thinking maybe I should buy a...
he pauses and then spells out G-U-N.
The girl sees her mother's eyes are red
like she's been crying,
but she's intrigued by what her father has said.
She says, *I know those letters, Daddy,*
and sounds out the word for him.
She senses she's right
and waits for their praise.

SEVERANCE

His wife is pregnant.
Nothing is so uncertain as this,
not even the old memories
of his insufficiency
when most needed.
It has haunted him,
that pool, early August sun,
the way a guitar case leans
precariously against a wall.
A slam can still make his muscles contract
as if he must push against gravity
into the malevolent air,
the water no more welcoming,
his skin the drag and weight against which
time is lost. How a body without life
feels in one's arms,
and now he will be expected to take into them
a newly animated one
that he is also responsible for,
will be asked to use a sharp tool
to sever the oxygenated line
to the inner pool in which,
he imagines,
the child has been safe,
and hold this child in this world
that has proven to him
the true meaninglessness of guardianship.
There are months and days to go yet.
She is growing happier.
Soon they will know the gender,
and his mouth goes dry
at the thought of a son,
his faith in failure,
both his own and the boy's.

SEA BRIGHT, SEA WALL

There, against the wide Atlantic,
holding it back from the main boulevard
and the homes of old-timers who call this their backyard,
they line the rocks,
knees drawn up, arms around each other
in small huddles,
the pellucid air allowing them to see
everything that is missing
across the Raritan bay—
empty spaces no one can agree on how to fill.

Once, it had been about light,
how it funneled up out of the ground
and entered the sky.
Now, they wait for the fireworks
that no longer mean anything but pleasure,
the accrual of sensation,
sound and sight, a pounding as if in a war,
not deafening at this distance, but enough.

One small family: the father covers his son's ears
as the boy trembles,
and whispers, *Look at the lights.*
The architecture of it—
synchronized lasers, water flumes, bursts, and flames.
Below them the ocean waves charge benignly,
the salt spray biting at their faces,
just a hint of chill
as the night floods in
to claim the shore,

and the father,
looking at what is reflected in his son's gaping face,
falls against the foot of the rock wall
he's been building all his life.

THE WAYS WATER IS USED

Her youngest daughter's thick curly hair
should not be washed every night;
she knows this,
but her daughter begs her to do it,
loves the ritual, the smell of the shampoo and cream rinse.
It is becoming a chore, the mother thinks,
the child getting big enough to do this herself.
Her own hair is a large knot of curls
kept at bay on the top of her brown forehead
by a plastic comb, the light streaks she has painted there
spiraling away like sweet pea in the garden
she keeps with her girls.
Every night, she folds the tea towel across her child's forehead
to keep the sprayed water from her eyes and face.
Don't drown me, Mama, the girl always teases
and they laugh, but tonight she hears the word from the news,
the one about the way water is used
to simulate drowning.
Her daughter's neck in her hand feels startlingly strong,
the eyes that look up at her disconcertingly wise,
and below them, the tub water shimmers
with foam infected with light,
reflecting it in pink and purple.
The daughter suddenly splashes her.
She lets the child go
and threatens to send her to her room for the night.
The girl goes under briefly and emerges sputtering,
wipes her face of suds,
and says, *If you try to send me to my room, I will fight you.*
The mother taught all three of her daughters to swim
by throwing them in the deep end.
It is how she learned herself.
What can she say to the child,
but *Come here; let me rinse you again.*

WHAT BREATHES AT THE OXYGEN BAR

They need very little oxygen,
will survive in austere waters fish have fled,
pollution's dimmed lights alright.
They thrive,
cockroaches of the ocean,
and when they closed the beach at Asbury
the second time that summer,
the boards swelled with unbuttoned teenagers
eyeing each other for tattoos, scars, other add-ons.
His almost ancient eyes
could spot the mixed breeds
in the evening mist ten storefronts down.
Above,
Tilly's round face,
saved from a tear-down,
welded in place.
The kids love it
and gather
and buy buttons for two bucks a piece.
Jellyfish, he calls the cream colored half white, half black kids with green eyes.
Moonpie, he whispers to the Koreans
even if they are Chinese or Thai.
Two girls working for him are Lithuanian.
My little sausages, he says.
This year everyone
seems thin and tending toward brown,
the water too warm, thick with debris,
the day business better than ever,
the night as it always is,
overcharged and fecund.

OXYGEN, MOON

The boy got away by climbing the fence
and hid in the shadows of the pool house,
the moon clothed in nomadic clouds
that would soon blow by.

He found the gate to the baby pool unlocked,
and opened and shut it
with only the smallest of grating sounds.

The others had been scared off by the signs
that read *These premises are always under surveillance.*

Above him,
a dark unlidded eye,
below,
the cool concrete,
and he lay down,
wondering who could see him.

Soon, the clouds raced on,
the big moon creeping across the pool's surface,
a jellyfish or stingray rippling
when the boy fanned his fingers
through the cold water.

When he was a baby,
then a toddler,
he'd played here.

At home, his mother
is counting the minutes until curfew,
and the boys who are after him are lingering
along the road home.

Here, below this breathing moon,
for a little while,
nothing is expected of him.

He puts his arm in the water up to the elbow,
his hand flat on the rough bottom
and breathes easily,
his shirt riding up exposing the basket of his ribs,

inspiring, expiring,

the membranes between water and air,

sky and ground
tender and grave
as a kiss.

RECENT TITLES FROM ALICE JAMES BOOKS

Milk Dress, Nicole Cooley
Parable of Hide and Seek, Chad Sweeney
Shahid Reads His Own Palm, Reginald Dwayne Betts
How to Catch a Falling Knife, Daniel Johnson
Phantom Noise, Brian Turner
Father Dirt, Mihaela Moscaliuc
Pageant, Joanna Fuhrman
The Bitter Withy, Donald Revell
Winter Tenor, Kevin Goodan
Slamming Open the Door, Kathleen Sheeder Bonanno
Rough Cradle, Betsy Sholl
Shelter, Carey Salerno
The Next Country, Idra Novey
Begin Anywhere, Frank Giampietro
The Usable Field, Jane Mead
King Baby, Lia Purpura
The Temple Gate Called Beautiful, David Kirby
Door to a Noisy Room, Peter Waldor
Beloved Idea, Ann Killough
The World in Place of Itself, Bill Rasmovicz
Equivocal, Julie Carr
A Thief of Strings, Donald Revell
Take What You Want, Henrietta Goodman
The Glass Age, Cole Swensen
The Case Against Happiness, Jean-Paul Pecqueur
Ruin, Cynthia Cruz
Forth A Raven, Christina Davis
The Pitch, Tom Thompson
Landscapes I & II, Lesle Lewis
Here, Bullet, Brian Turner
The Far Mosque, Kazim Ali
Gloryland, Anne Marie Macari
Polar, Dobby Gibson
Pennyweight Windows: New & Selected Poems, Donald Revell
Matadora, Sarah Gambito
In the Ghost-House Acquainted, Kevin Goodan

Alice James Books has been publishing poetry since 1973 and remains one of the few presses in the country that is run collectively. The cooperative selects manuscripts for publication primarily through regional and national annual competitions. Authors who win a Kinereth Gensler Award become active members of the cooperative board and participate in the editorial decisions of the press. The press, which historically has placed an emphasis on publishing women poets, was named for Alice James, sister of William and Henry, whose fine journal and gift for writing went unrecognized during her lifetime.

TYPESET AND DESIGNED BY MARY AUSTIN SPEAKER

Printed by Thomson-Shore

on 30% postconsumer recycled paper

processed chlorine-free